25 Bilingual Mini-Books

Easy-to-Make Books for Emergent Readers,
in English and Spanish

by
Helen H. Moore and Jaime Lucero

SCHOLASTIC
PROFESSIONAL BOOKS

NEW YORK • TORONTO • LONDON • AUCKLAND • SYDNEY

Dedication

To Jimmy and Pattie, "brother and sister of the daughter of *Machiste*" — Helen

A mi madre, con todo amor y cariño — Jaime

Acknowledgments

Thanks to Terry Cooper, who knows how to give chances, as well as take them.

Copyright © 1994 Helen H. Moore and Jaime Lucero
Designed by Carmen Robert Sorvillo
Cover design by Vincent Ceci
Cover and interior illustration by Robert Alley
Cover photograph by Donnelly Marks

12 11 10 9 8 7   678/9
ISBN 0-590-49802-9

Contents ....

Introduction

This collection of mini-books builds on the foundation laid by several other books, also published by Scholastic, entitled *25 Thematic Mini-Books, 25 Mother Goose Peek-a-Books,* and *25 Science Mini-Books.* Since I enjoyed working on the other books in the series so much, whether as an author (Mother Goose), or as an editor, and since teachers had been letting us know how much they and their students enjoyed these little books, writing a new selection of mini-books seemed inevitable. But what topic should the new selection center around?

It would have to be something teachers could really use, that would enrich their practice while remaining child-pleasing and fresh. Jaime Lucero and I considered many topics, until he came back from the National Association of Bilingual Educators Conference with a great idea. "We have to offer more bilingual materials," he said. He'd seen that the need was great. And that's how *25 Bilingual Mini-Books* got its start.

These mini-books have been designed to be easy to make and easy to read, with a child-pleasing focus on food, family, neighborhood, animals, and weather. They should help to encourage both emergent and fluent readers, and can be made more or less interactive by the amount of preparation you invite from the children: they can color the books, or add text or drawings. Of course the folding and cutting of the books makes certain that hands-on involvement is an integral part of the reading experience: but if you wish, you or a parent volunteer can make enough mini-books for all the students to read, and have them ready before class begins. It's all up to you.

A Word on Bilingual Education

While we recognize that there is no true consensus on the goal of bilingual education, we also recognize that there are some areas on which most segments of the population agree: Namely, that in our society, there are large numbers of immigrants for whom English is not the native tongue, and the largest number of these new Americans are native Spanish speakers. In the main, they wish to become assimilated and to participate in the dominant culture without forgetting their culture or language of origin. The children of these new Americans need literacy materials to help them make the transition from their mother tongue that are child-centered, developmentally appropriate, interactive, and motivating, just as native English speakers do.

We offer these 25 bilingual mini-books in the hope that they will help teachers in their efforts to make the transition to English as gentle and positive an experience for their students as possible.

Using the Mini-Books ....

There are many ways to use these books, once you've mastered making them! If you've never used a mini-book pattern before, there's a key phrase that it will pay to bear in mind: "If at first you don't succeed, try, try, again."

As you would with any new instructional material or skill, try making a few of the books yourself, outside of class, while preparing your lessons.

A little experimentation with a double-sided copier will help: every copier is different, and you will need to find out how to position both the original and the copy in order to align the type on both sides of each mini-book page.

When you start using the mini-books with the class (and be advised: these little books provoke a lot of interest when students see them for the first time), you may wish to read one book to the group first, and then distribute the copies so they can make their own mini-books! It helps to model the steps for them first, and then invite them to follow along. We've tried to keep the folding and cutting to a minimum, bearing in mind the developing motor skills of the primary student. Once you've got the books folded, they're ready to read.

Of course, students will enjoy having you lead them in making the books and then reading the stories in large or small groups, to each other, or individually. The topics of the books are consistent with commonly-taught themes in the primary grades; use the books to extend theme studies. They can be part of a fun way to encourage parent involvement: copy the directions and send them home along with a copy of one of the mini-books for a motivating homework assignment. When students have mastered making some of the simpler books, you may want to make copies of several books and place a stack at a learning center for students to make and read independently. You will probably have your own favorite way of using them, and we wish you as much enjoyment (and learning) as we had in creating them.

– Helen H. Moore

– Jaime Lucero

Directions ....

These peek-a-books have been arranged in order of complexity: from the very simple, one-fold books, to those that require folding, cutting, and, in a few cases, gluing or taping. This is simply because we had to order the books *some* way: we hope you will use them in any order that fits your and your students' needs and interests. You are the expert in regard to your own class, and you know best the level of ease or difficulty your students experience when cutting, folding and pasting are required.

We have tried to make these books as interactive as possible by inviting the children to add text or illustrations of their own to some of them. You may wish to encourage them to color the line drawings, and even to make their own mini-books after they have mastered the format.

Note: Each of the following directions is designed to be made with a single 8½" x 11" sheet of standard copy paper.

> For all the books, dotted lines are fold lines, and solid lines are for cutting. **Important:** For best results, remove each bilingual mini-book at the perforations, and copy on a copier with double-sided capability. If this isn't possible, copy the first page of any given mini-book on a regular copier, then replace the copies in the feeder tray with the blank side up. Remove the first page from the platen glass and place the second page there. You may need to experiment a few times to discover the proper alignment of the pages, but with a little patience you will find the results are worth it, as children love these motivating, inexpensive little books.

First, invite students to hold the 8½" x 11" paper vertically, with the short sides parallel to the floor and ceiling of the room, and the long sides parallel to the walls of the classroom. Invite them to look for the dotted fold lines and/or the solid cut lines, and help them understand what they are to do on these lines.

I. One-Fold Books: *Miguelito the Mouse, Class Picnic, Happy Birthday, Outside Our Window,* and *Let's Paint*

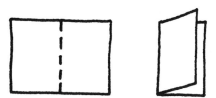

Simply: fold the book along the dotted fold line, and you're ready to read. With the *Happy Birthday* and *Class Picnic* books, the children can enjoy holding the third page up to the window and looking "inside" the piñata and the lunch bag.

II. Two-Fold Books: *The Four Seasons, Look in the Mirror, Fruit Salad, One Little Teddy Bear,* and *The Circus*

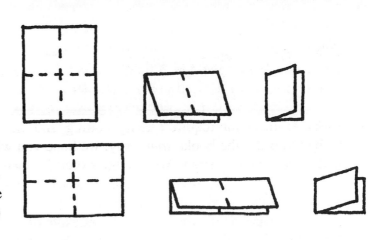

For all except the *The Circus* book, simply:
1. Fold the paper along the dotted horizontal fold line, then
2. Fold it in half again along the vertical fold line to form the mini-book. (For *The Circus*, reverse the order of the folds: vertical first, then horizontal.)

III. Three-Fold Books: *Let's Go to the Supermarket* and *Let's Go to School*

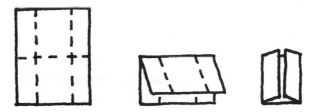

1. Fold paper in half along the dotted line.
2. With the image facing you, fold each side (along the dotted lines) towards the center.

IV. Multiple Fold Books:

Welcome to Our Show

1. Hold paper vertically, with the inside facing you. Fold in half.
2. You should be looking at the front cover (image is of theatre curtain with text: *Welcome to Our Show/Bienvenido a Nuestra Función*).
3. To read, fold the front page up from the bottom on the dotted lines, one section at a time, to slowly reveal the characters from foot to head.

Little Snake, Little Snake

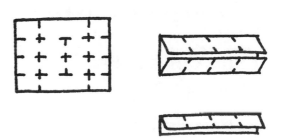

1. Hold paper horizontally, with the large image of the sick snake facing you.
2. Fold the top and bottom strips along the dotted lines toward the middle as shown.
3. Fold the folded paper in half, enclosing the opening inside, as shown.

4. Fold the resulting strip (through all thicknesses) into quarters on the dotted lines in accordian style, as shown. Unfold in reverse order to read.

Families

1. Hold the paper vertically, with the full-page, single image facing you, right side up. Note the three vertical fold lines that divide the paper into quarters.
2. Fold the extreme right and left quarters of the paper toward the center.
3. Then fold in half along the center fold line as shown. You should now have a folded strip of paper one fourth as wide as you started with.
4. Turn it so that the folded edge is on your left, and the open edge is on your right.
5. Then fold the top and bottom quarters toward you, so the edges meet in the center, as shown.
6. Fold in half once more. The front "cover" of the book has the first line of the rhyme on it. Unfold in the reverse order to read.

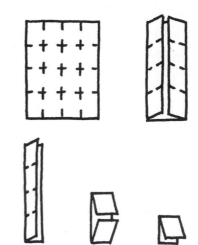

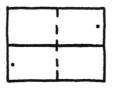

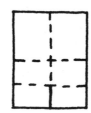

V. Accordion Fold Books:

The Elephant

1. Cut the paper in half along the solid cut line.
2. Attach the edges marked with dots (•) to each other with tape or glue.
3. Fold like an accordion, as shown, with the page numbered 1 on top.

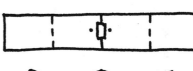

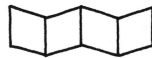

VI. Fold and Cut Books:

Animals and Their Babies

Make two, simple, greeting card-type folds on the dotted fold lines, and cut on the solid cut line.

Where Do Animals Live?

1. Hold paper horizontally and fold on the dotted line.
2. Cut on the three solid lines as shown.

Little Cricket

1. Hold paper vertically and fold the top and bottom towards the center on dotted lines.
2. Cut the two solid lines in the top half. See diagram at right.
3. Fold again on dotted line as indicated in diagram at right.
4. Fold once more on dotted line as shown at right. Image should be facing you.

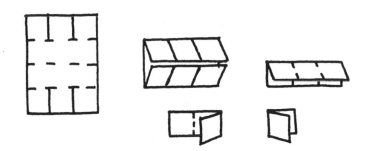

VII. Diamond Cut Books: *One Week*
and *The Cat and the Dog*

1. Fold the long edges of the paper to meet. Crease well and unfold.
2. Then fold the short edges of the paper to meet. Crease well, and *do not unfold*.
3. Holding the unfolded paper, fold the right side over to meet the left side. Crease well.
4. Unfold the last fold you just made. Cut on the fold along the cut line, being careful only to cut as far as indicated. Unfold. The opened page will have eight creased sections and a slit in the center.
5. Fold the long edges over to meet, as in step one.
6. Hold the folded side edges together, and gently push the paper inward to form a book.
7. The center cut opens out in a diamond shape as you fold it, before coming together again and flattening out, giving the cut its name.

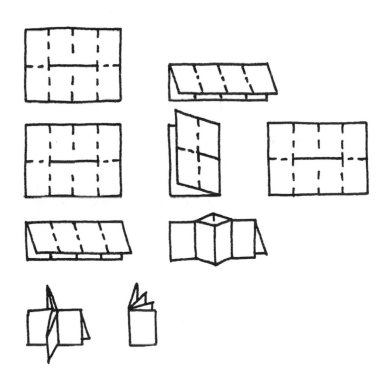

VIII. Pinch Fold Pop-Up Books:

The Bird and *The Frog*

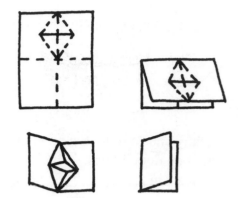

1. Fold the paper in half on the long fold line and crease well.
2. Cut on the solid line.
3. You will have to experiment with pushing the angled fold line in; pinching the paper on each side of the fold line seems to work well. The angle of the fold determines the degree of "pop" in your pop-up.
4. Crease well once you have the paper folded the way you want. The better the crease, the better the pop up.
5. Open the page and push the flaps through to the other side. Close the book and you're ready to read.

• •

IX. Sliders: *What Do We Wear?*
and *Transportation*

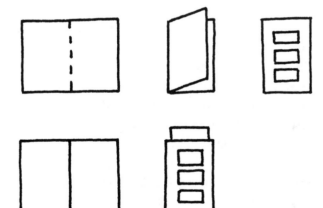

Slider Book Holder:
1. Hold paper horizontally and fold in half (on dotted line) so that images face you.
2. To cut boxes out, cut along solid lines.
3. Tape side of sheet along the long edge.

Slider Sheet:
4. Cut page 59 in half (on solid line). Note: There are two sliders on this page, one for each slider book.
5. Insert each slider sheet into its appropriate holder.

Hello!
I'm Miguelito.

¡Hola!
Soy Miguelito.

Mmmm.
Shapes can be very tasty!

Mmmm.
¡Las formas geométricas pueden ser muy sabrosas!

Will you help me look for triangles, rectangles, circles and squares?

¿Me ayudas a buscar triángulos, rectángulos, círculos y cuadrados?

Let's go on a class picnic.

We bring our lunches with us. Our teacher puts all our food in one big bag.

Vamos a un día de campo con la clase.

Todos traemos nuestra propia comida. La maestra pone toda la comida en una bolsa grande.

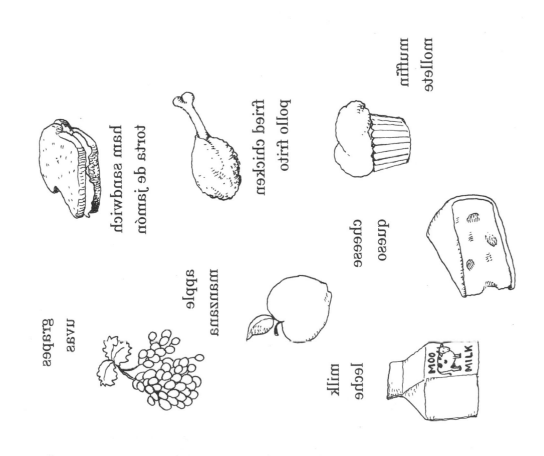

ham sandwich
torta de jamón

fried chicken
pollo frito

muffin
mollete

cheese
queso

apple
manzana

grapes
uvas

milk
leche

I brought a banana, a sandwich, some cookies, and some juice. I wonder what everyone else brought?

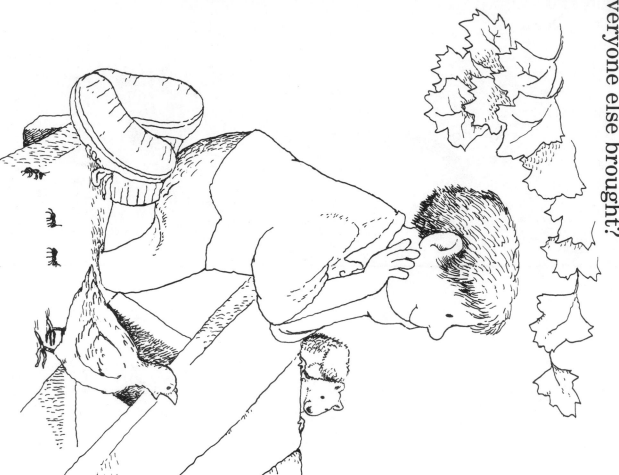

Yo traje un plátano, una torta, unas galletas, y jugo. ¿Qué traerían los demás?

Hold this page up to a window and see what's in the big bag.

Deten esta página sobre una ventana para ver qué hay adentro de la bolsa grande.

Happy Birthday!

It's my birthday...
I invite you to my party.

¡Feliz Cumpleaños!

Es mi cumpleaños...
Te invito a mi fiesta.

No quiero oro
Ni quiero plata
yo lo que quiero
es quebrar la piñata.

–Spanish traditional rhyme

I don't want gold
I don't want silver
I just want
to break the piñata.

We'll have fun with my piñata.
When it breaks, we'll have a surprise!

¡Nos divertiremos con mi piñata.
Cuando la rompamos, tendremos
una sopresa!

Hold this page up to a window
to see the surprises inside the piñata.

Detén esta página sobre una ventana
para ver las sopresas adentro de la piñata.

Come and see what's
outside the window!

¡Ven a ver que hay
afuera de la ventana!

Look out your window. What do you see?
Draw it here.

Ve afuera de la ventana. ¿Qué ves?
Dibújalo aquí.

Let's Paint

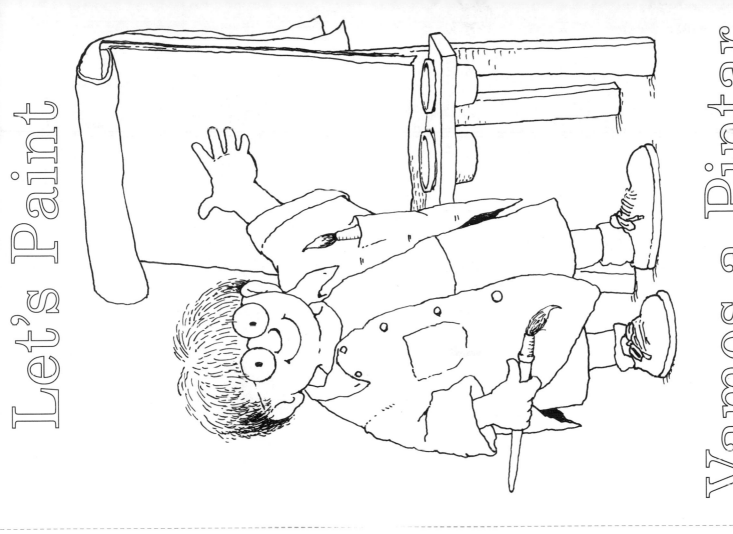

Vamos a Pintar

The sky is blue.
The grass is green.
The sun is yellow.
The apples are red.

Draw yourself playing in this scene.
Then add your favorite colors.

El cielo es azul.
El césped es verde.
El sol es amarillo.
Las manzanas son rojas.

Dibújate jugando en este escenario.
Y luego usa tus colores favoritos.

En el invierno, la nieve puede caer de las nubes.

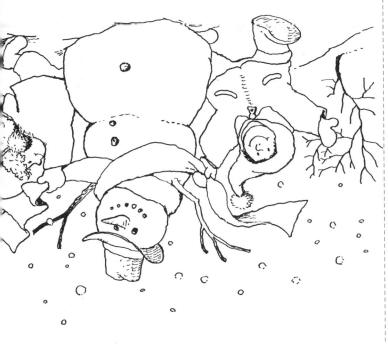

In winter, snow can fall from the clouds.

En el otoño, vamos al escuela.

In the fall, we go to school.

And in the spring, flowers begin to bloom.

Y en la primavera, las flores empiezan a florecer.

The Four Seasons
In summer, we have fun under the sun!

Las Cuatro Estaciones
¡En el verano, nos divertimos bajo del sol!

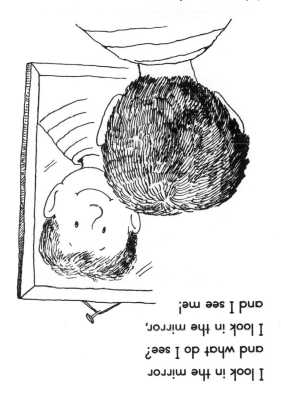

Me veo en el espejo.
¿Y qué es lo que veo?
Me veo en el espejo.
¡Y me veo yo!

I look in the mirror
and what do I see?
I look in the mirror,
and I see me!

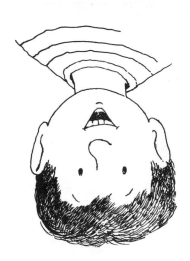

una nariz, dos orejas, dos cejas también;
dos labios, y dientes,
para decir "Te amo."

Un par de ojos me ven;

A pair of eyes looks back at me;
a nose, two ears, two eyebrows, too;
two lips, and teeth,
to say "I love you."

What do you see when you look in the mirror? Use this page to draw what you see.

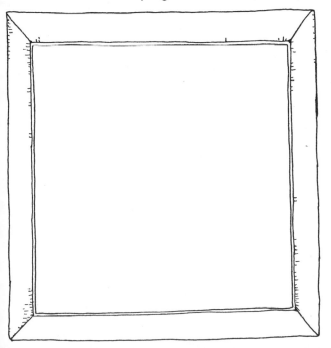

¿Qué es lo que ves cuando te ves en el espejo?
Usa esta página para dibujar lo que ves.

I look in the mirror...
And what do I see?

Me veo en el espejo...
Y qué es lo que veo?

¿Me ayudas a hacer una ensalada de fruta?

Will you help me make a fruit salad?

Necesitaremos:

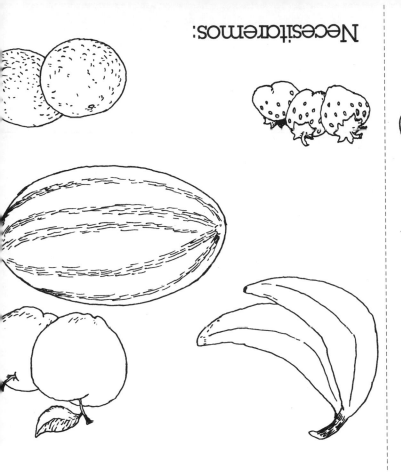

We'll need:

Fruit Salad

I eat fruit every day.

Ensalada de Fruta

Yo como fruta todos los días.

I'll get stronger if I eat fruit every day.
Draw fruit in the bowl.

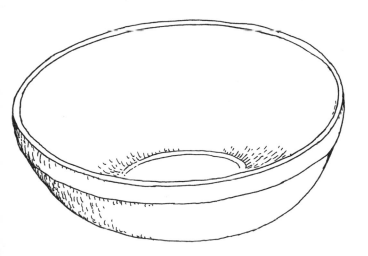

Me pondré más fuerte si como fruta todos los días.
Dibuja la fruta en el tazón.

Otro osito vino,
luego eran tres.

Another little bear came,
and then there were three.

Three little teddy bears
to play with me.
Draw a picture of yourself playing with the teddy bears.

Tres ositos de juguete
para jugar conmigo.
Dibuja un retrato de tí mismo(a) jugando con los ositos de juguete.

Dos ositos de juguete
sentados en un árbol.

Two little teddy bears
sitting in a tree.

One Little Teddy Bear

One little teddy bear
lonely as can be.

Un Osito de Juguete

Un osito de juguete
tan solito como puede estar.

Los osos son grandes.

The bears are big.

Los payasos son más grandes.

The clowns are bigger.

Los elefantes son los más grandes.

The elephants are the biggest.

The Circus Comes to Town

The animals and acrobats make a parade.

El Circo Viene al Pueblo

Los animales y los acróbatas hacen un desfile.

And here they all are!

¡Y aquí están todos!

El gerente nos saluda.

The manager says hello.

Supermarket

Supermercado

Draw healthy foods inside the cart.

Dibuja comidas saludables en la carreta.

Let's Go to th

Vamos a

Can you help us find healthy foods?

¿Nos aydudas a buscar comida saludable?

Nuestros padres vienen de visita.

Abre la página para ver nuestra aula.

Open the page to see our classroom.

Our parents come to visit.

ur school.

uestra escuela.

We love

Queremos a

Welcome to our show!

Where we will learn about the body.

¡Bienvenido a nuestra función!

Donde aprenderemos del cuerpo.

You will see feet,

⇩

knees,

⇩

hands, arms,
and tummies.

⇩

And heads,
of course!

Verás pies,

rodillas,

manos, brazos,
y pancitas.

¡Y cabezas,
claro!

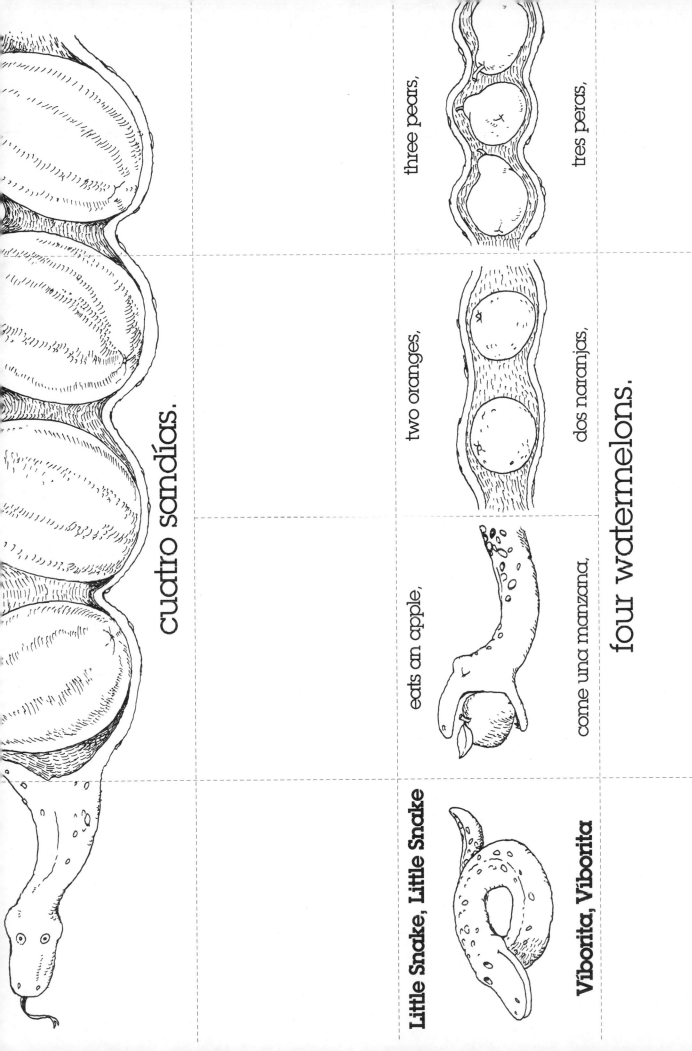

cuatro sandías.

three pears,

tres peras,

two oranges,

dos naranjas,

four watermelons.

eats an apple,

come una manzana,

Little Snake, Little Snake

Viborita, Viborita

Poor little snake now has a tummy ache.

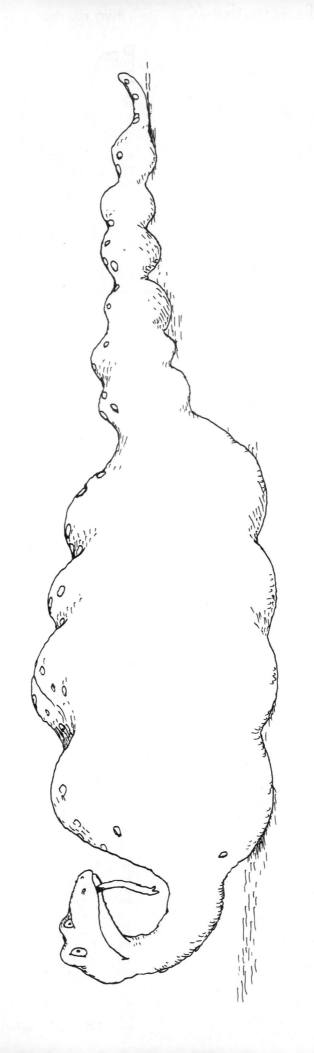

Pobrecita víborita ahora tiene dolor de estomaguito.

My stepmother loves me.

Mi madrastra me quiere.

A mother, a baby brother... Una mamá, y un hermanito...

---

an uncle...

un tío...

I have a father.

Tengo un papá.

I live with my grandma.

Vivo con mi abuela.

I have a sister... Familias Tengo una hermana... Families

Families

---

grandma and grandpa...

abuela y abuelo...

I have three sisters.

Tengo tres hermana

My brother is my best friend.

Mi hermano es mi mejor amigo.

Draw a picture of your family here.

Dibuja a tu familia aquí.

---

some cousins...

algunos primos...

I love my stepfather.

Quiero a mi padrastro.

I live with my dad and our pets.

¡Vivo con mi papá y nuestras mascotas!

---

two aunties... dos tías...

---

and some friends.

y algunos amigos.

I have lots of cousin

Tengo muchos prim

There are many different kinds of families
living together in our big world!

¡Hay muchas clases diferentes de familias
viviendo juntas en nuestro gran mundo!

on a s[p]ider's web one day.

en la tela de una araña,

she called for another elephant to come.

fue a llamar a otro elefante.

An elep ant went out to play...

Un elefante se balanceaba...

She had such enormous fun...

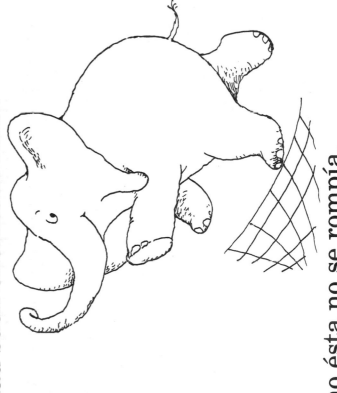

y como ésta no se rompía,

"Three elephants went out to play,
on a spider's web one day.

Tres elefantes se balanceaban
en la tela de una araña.

Two elephants went out to play,
on a spider's web one day.

Dos elefantes se balanceaban
en la tela de una araña,

The spider came along to say…
"You'll break my web! Now go away!!"

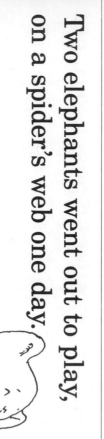

Y la araña vino a decir…
"¡Van a romper mi tela! ¡Ahora váyanse!"

They had such enormous fun,
they called for another elephant to come!

y como ésta no se rompía,
fueron a llamar a otro elefante.

¡puppies!
¡cachorritos!

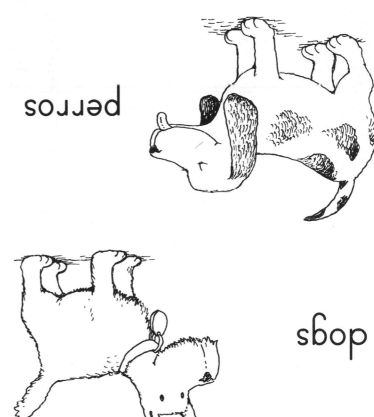

perros

dogs

bears

osos

Animals and their Babies
Los animales y sus Bebés

cat   gato

¡gatitos!

kittens!

¡ositos!

cubs!

Where do animals live?

¿Donde viven los animales?

Who lives
in the desert?

¿Quién vive
en el desierto?

Who lives
in the forest?

¿Quién vive
en el bosque?

Who lives
on the farm?

¿Quién vive
en la granja?

Who lives
in the ocean?

¿Quién vive
en el océano?

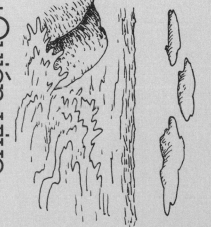

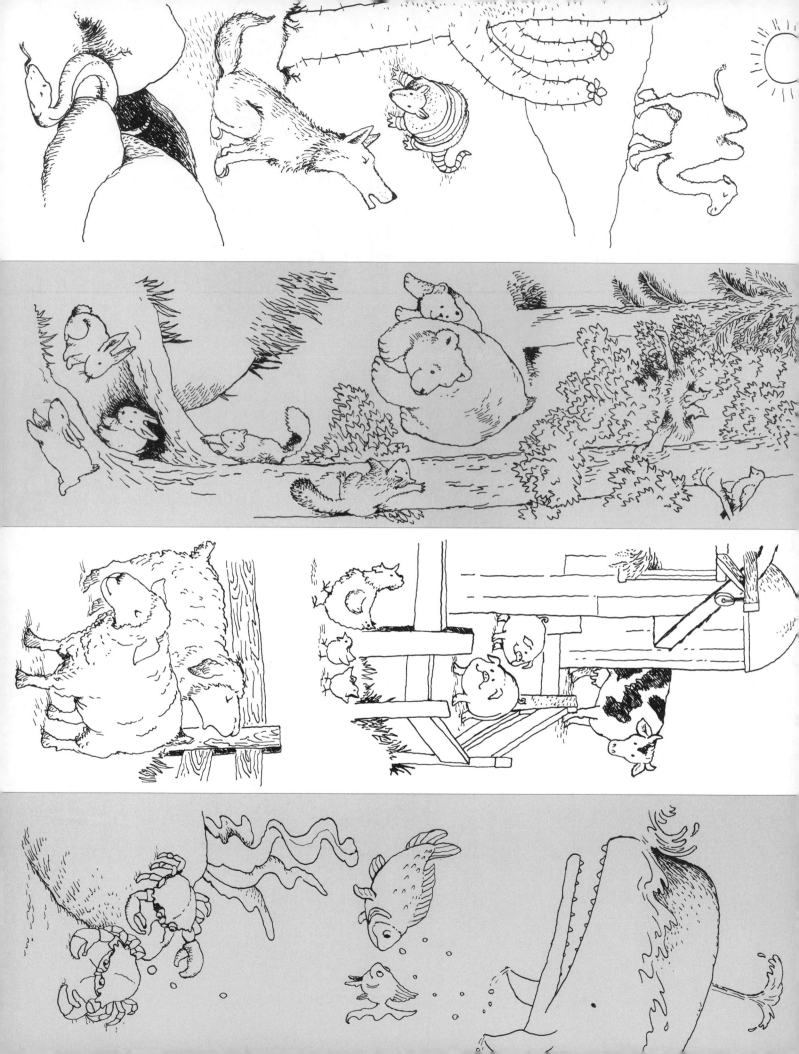

¿Fuiste tu
Clara?

¿Fuiste tu
Antonio?

¿Fuiste tu
Lupita?

A frog in the pond swallowed my friend

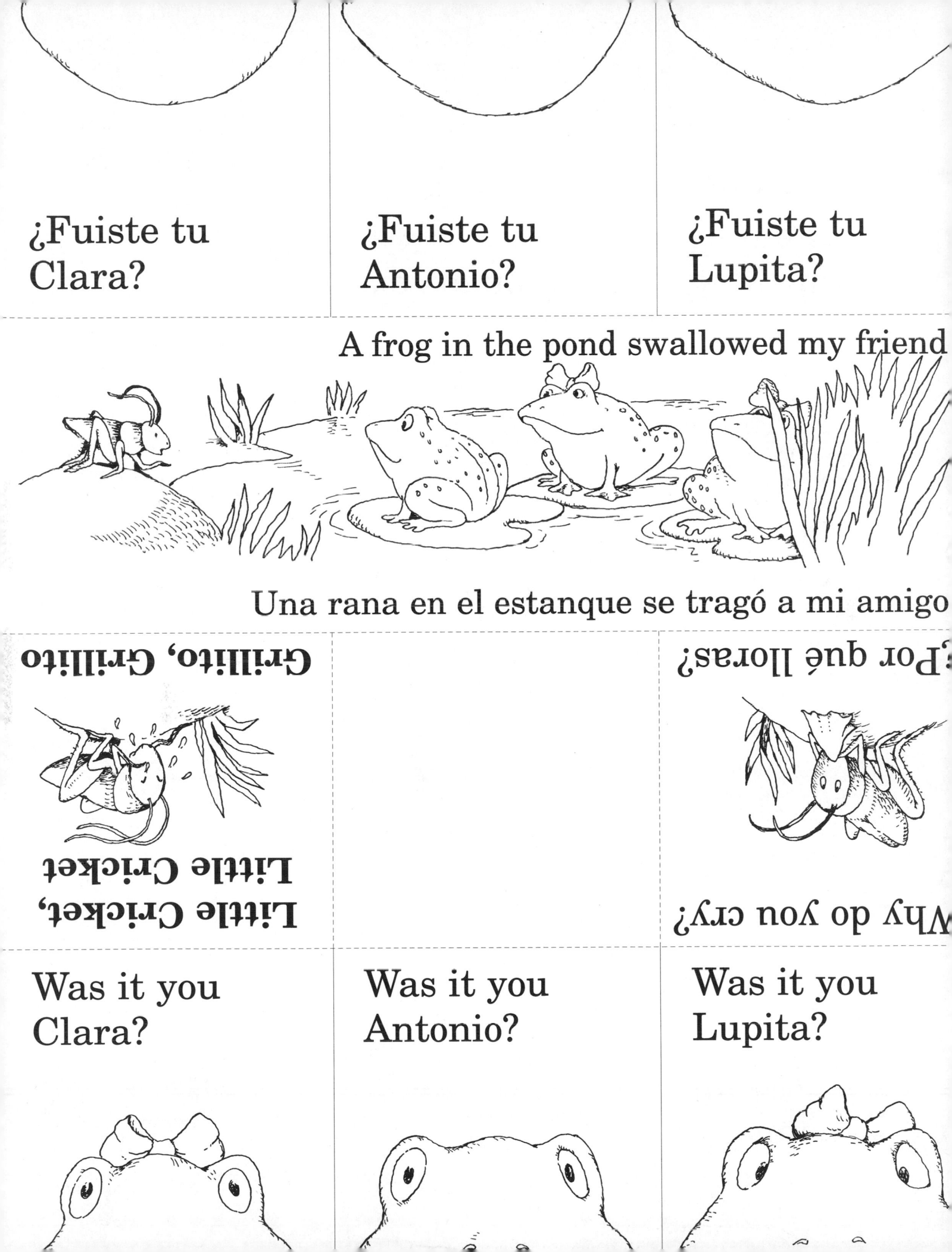

Una rana en el estanque se tragó a mi amigo

Grillito, Grillito

¿Por qué lloras?

Little Cricket,
Little Cricket

Why do you cry?

Was it you
Clara?

Was it you
Antonio?

Was it you
Lupita?

No, it was not me. | No, it was not me. | Yes, it was me.
I swallowed th
fly.

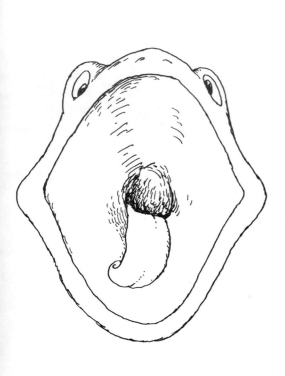 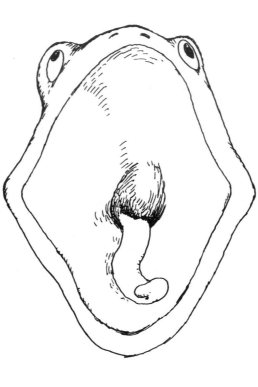 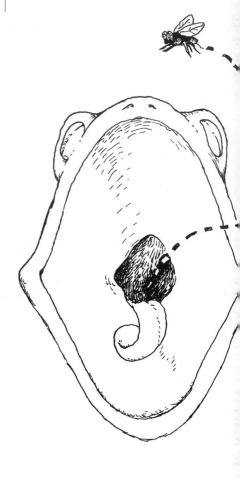

No, yo no fuí. | No, yo no fuí. | Sí, yo fuí.
Yo me tragué la
mosca.

One Week

Una Semana

On Monday,
I go to school.

El lunes,
(voy a la escuela)

On Tuesday,
I play.

El martes,
(juego)

On Wednesday,
I watch t.v.

El miércoles,
(veo televisión)

On Thursday,
I read a book.

El jueves,
(leo un libro)

On Sunday,
I rest.

El domingo,
descanso.

On Saturday,
I go to the zoo.

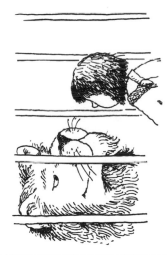

El sábado, voy
al zoológico.

On Friday,
I sleep at my
friend's house.

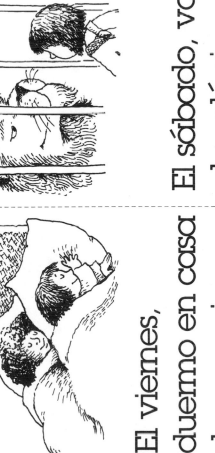

El viernes,
duermo en casa
de un amigo.

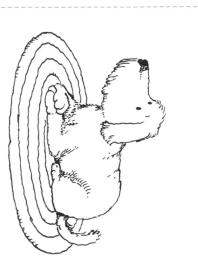

"Es hora
de ir al pueblo."

"It's time
to go to town."

The cat came down
the stairs and
said.

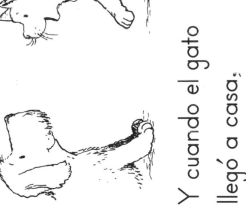

El
gato bajó los
escalones y dijo

El perro dijo, "No
quiero ir.

The dog said, "I don't
want to go,

they both did what
they liked the best.

los dos hicieron
lo que más les gusta.

Me quedaré y me
echaré aquí."

I'll stay here and lie
down."

And when the cat
came home

Y cuando el gato
llegó a casa,

El gato salió y
se divirtió

The cat went out and
had some fun...

The dog stayed home
to rest...

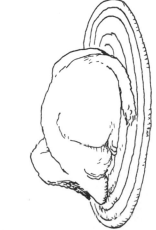

El perro se quedó en
casa para descansar...

Es un pajarito, esperando que le den de comer.

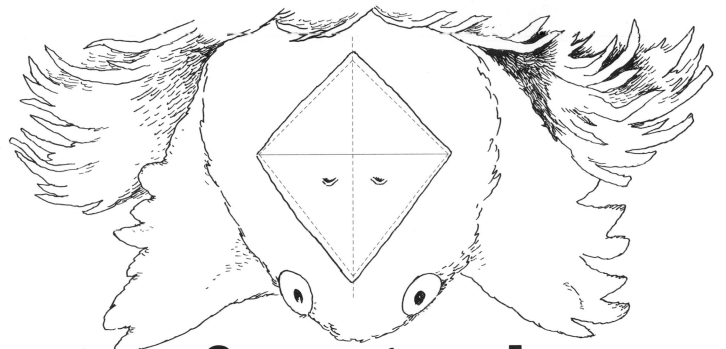

It's a baby bird, waiting to be fed.

Good for you, mama bird!

¡Enhorabuena, mamá pájaro!

Early in the morning, while I'm trying to sleep, I hear a noise outside my window.

Temprano en la mañana, mientras trato de dormir, oigo un ruido afuera de mi ventana.

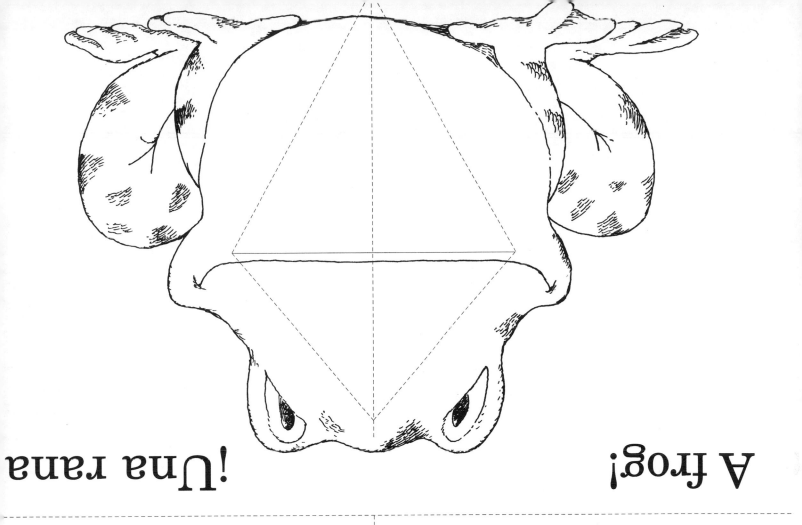

¡Una rana!

A frog!

Use this page to draw a frog.

**Over in the forest,
in a pond so deep,
lives a little green something
that can really leap.**

**Allá en el bosque,
en una charca honda,
vive algo chiquito y verde
que de verdad puede brincar.**

Dibuja una rana en esta página.

What clothes do we wear?

When it's hot we can wear:

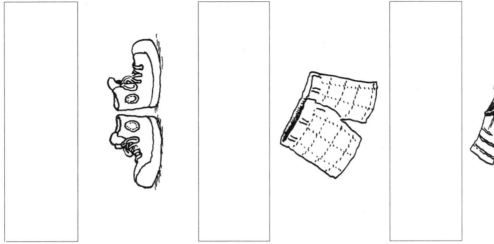

Cuando hace calor podemos usar:

¿Que ropa nos ponemos?

Cuando llueve, necesitamos:

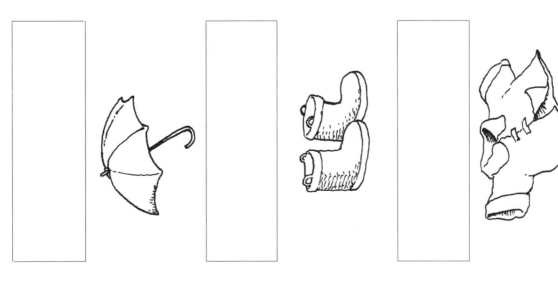

When it's raining, we need:

zapatos de lona

sneakers

pantalones cortos

shorts

camisa

shirt

un avión

a plane

un tren

a train

un autobús

a bus

an umbrella

un paraguas

boots

botas

a raincoat

un impermeable

a bicycle

una bicicleta

a boat

un barco

a car

un auto

Transportation

When we want to go somewhere, we can take:

   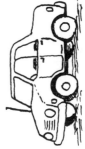 

Transportación

Cuando queremos ir a un lugar podemos tomar un:

  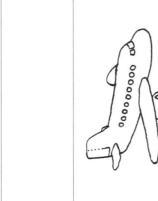  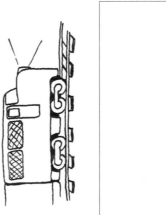